ARTIFACTS
POEMS

by

Paul Skuta

DORRANCE
PUBLISHING CO
EST. 1920
PITTSBURGH, PENNSYLVANIA 15238

"The beasts in Lascaux huddle" was published previously in The Michigan Quarterly Review. "The season has descended" was published previously under the title, "Descent," in *Pivot*, a journal of The Poetry Workshop of the Pennsylvania State University.

Dorrance Publishing Co
585 Alpha Drive
Suite 103
Pittsburgh, PA 15238
Visit our website at www. dorrancebookstore.com

ISBN: 979-8-89027-291-1
eISBN: 979-8-89027-789-3

for Carole Sue

INTRODUCTION

I know only generally when it happened but I know exactly how.

I would have been barely school age when, occasionally at bedtime, my mother would read to me from a big book with a shiny, red cover. At least, it seemed big to me. It was certainly red. Very shiny, very red. In the center of the very shiny, very red back cover, which I could see as my mother held up the book to read, was a smiling and winking, yellow crescent moon. When she finished reading a story or a poem from the book, she would close it, then hold the back cover under the bedroom lamp. By jiggling the book back and forth under the lamp, she made the moon seem to dance.

No wonder then that I expected magic to come out of that book. And it did. One bedtime she read me a poem about Halloween. In the poem was "a big, red moon rolling up the hill." Whenever that particular bedtime was is when it happened and that is exactly how I discovered the magic of poetry. Someone I would never know had put words together in a special way so that they became an incantation. When the words were repeated they had the power to leave the page and make me see the moon as I had never seen it before. I wanted to do magic like that, too. I wanted to be a magician.

I began to devise incantations of my own. By the third grade I was practiced enough to feel, for one of the few times since, full confidence to meet a challenge. My third-grade teacher, Mrs. Holsopfel, a motherly and encouraging woman, was introducing our class to poetry. She read aloud some simple verses and we talked about them. Then she asked each of us to compose a poem of our own for the next day. Finally, a subject that, unlike long division, caused me no anxiety and did not make the back of my neck prickle.

Whatever I came up with in response to that assignment, mercifully, is lost to time but Mrs. Holsopfel liked it. She asked if I could write another one. I liked Mrs. Holsopfel and didn't want to disappoint her.

That very evening I knocked out something and presented it to her the next day. It was good, she said, but not as good as the first one. She said I could to better.

Like the other teachers, I imagine, Mrs, Holsopfel served as a bus monitor, too. Every morning she was there to help children off the bus and into the building. When it was me she happened to be helping, she would ask if I had a poem for her. I didn't always, but when I did, she was a gentle and fair critic.

As I look back, it seems to me that dear Mrs. Holsopfel's expression of genuine interest did more than merely nudge me in a direction. It set me at a trailhead for a path which would wind from there to here and promise at every turn to lead to that perfect magic spell.

Compiling this collection has been a sort of archaeological dig, an excavation of fifty years of incantations. Some were carefully preserved in journals; others were scratched haphazardly on napkins and the backs of envelopes. Some lay right at the surface, others long buried and forgotten. Their chronology came to matter less than their content.

And what of the mind and hands that fashioned these spells? They are a varied lot. Are they all the work of the same magician? Was he a magician at all; do the incantations work?

Try them.

I am sincerely grateful to Mr. J. B. Smith for his patient assistance in the preparation of this collection.

P.S.
2022

I
SKETCHES

The beasts in Lascaux huddle,
limp, mud hair
painted motionless in agony,
damp in fear,
watching from the walls
should the hunters come,
ready, if discovered,
to run.

winter 1973

a
b outt   o
w henthe   win db
lew (h
            erea
                        re) w
e(we)re w
e we   r e

autumn 1976 (10-18)

The blind pariah
hears you go,
listens from his cup.
His cup is hollow.
Hollow rings of
widening zero,
zero say no
no, say no.

autumn 1975 (11-6)

in the bare branches
of dawn-silhouetted trees
a painted silk scarf

winter 2019 (3-3)

II
COMMENTARIES

modern times

It's a mother
yes, but
it's just a cat.
It sits
beside kittens
(all ground up)
licking its paw
until
Whumpthumpwhumpthump,
lump. Well.
So what
's a car to do?

winter 2017 (1-7)

Man
we have, I guess,
arrived,
telling
(like labels list
ingredients)
our feelings in
New and Improved
terminology.
It is significant,
ABC Newsworthy,
like Band-Aids in colors,
The New Coke.

summer 1985

April

There is no cruelty.

Simply, the sun has warmed the same, old stones,
so that now, in a bite we have yet to take,
night air swims among some trunks
in what could be moonlight
but is the glow from the Miracle Mile.

Clearly the stars are real.

From water we have yet to drink or spit out,
voices rise high all night
but do not cross traffic.

Something nudges the litter.

Tomorrow we shall eat of this place,
drink the water,
spit it out
without asking to be
or even knowing that we are
forgiven.

spring 1994 (4-12)

The wives in Carthage
worried on their beds.
The Roman mothers wept
that such a time could come.
Later, when the fields
were buried in the dead,
they went out to bear
the standards home.

winter 1973

III
COMMUNICATION

Upon reading that, within weeks of August 6, 1945, radiation had roused millions of seeds, dormant in Hiroshima's soil, to send wild-flowers out of the city's ashes....

    Hiroshima suddenly is
    nothing
    (Power is partly
    surprise.
    It is
    not spring.)
    but poppies.
    (Party size.)

winter 1975

Je
sus&mary's
it - ting
in a tree,
K
yiyess - ess !
 i ? n ?
Gee.

winter 2001 (2-17)

Paul Skuta

The aster notices
the cold,
ignores the flakes—
a few.
This dignity delights
the snow.
It pretends aloofness,
too.

spring 1973

2 hu
m (almost)
a (ll) n
s pass
st (if) F
whose arms
(vinyl)
kisz

autumn 1980 (11-19)

Christmas Prayer

Behold,
Of Clear Celestial Eye;
uphold,
Of Perfect Hands, untie;
illuminate,
O Love of Light and My
Eternal;
open me.

autumn 2008 (11-25)

IV
LOVE

Love, like a flower,
might—suppose—and—hesitate,
bend, and—almost bloom—
then wait;
decide in the passing
of a hurried heart
then open—
late.

winter 1971

Love goes unattended
like a star.
Small. Self-sure
as a sound.
How proud the hearts
of lovers are—
like plovers, quick, demure
and skittering off the ground.

winter 1971

My heart, a huge,
well, paper;
kisses, kisses,
a kiss;
the words of Adam
in the voice of Pan.
Diamonds. Violets.
This.

winter 1988 (2-14)

Valentine Fable

Dragonfly with wings of spangle,
over steeple, under tangle,
prize of purple.

Boy with net, heart with simple
love of girl. Girl with giggle.
Hope eternal.

Prize and giggle, net and bramble.
Afternoon with sunlight sprinkle.
Hug and nuzzle.

Boy with girl, eyes with sparkle.
Dragonfly with wings of spangle.
All immortal.

winter 1994 (2-14)

What's forever
March romancing;
what's, at last,
a sea?
April; air. Then
who is dancing
with you&forever?
Me.

summer 2003 (6-15)

My Favorite Cup

When I hold you
I am never careless,
although the thin, gold rim,
your halo, is intact,
and even shinier
since you no longer hold anything
extreme or dark.
You were always too fine for that.
Your value is in holding nothing
but light.

My chipped cup,
my world-worn vessel
and perfect prize,
all else I relinquish
but you
I am taking with me.

autumn 1999 (9-16)

Bhakti

You enchant me
as spring scatters flowers,
as butterfly wings
sprinkle colors.

You anoint me
as light a hollow;
as you climb,
I follow.

You bewilder me
as marsh birds sing,
as the sun strikes the sea,
shattering.

You draw me
as grasses the dew;
You absorb me.
I become you.

winter 2000 (2-23)

s(he)

It is s(he) of the eyes
that see me,
(s)he of the hands
that touch me,
s(he) of the arms
that embrace me,
(s)he of the body
that joins me,
s(he) of the blood
that warms me,
(s)he of the mind
that knows me,
s(he) of the love
that draws me
to the (s)he of the you
that is me.

autumn 2009 (10-18)

I went there today
where once we picked Narcissi.
Changed. But there were some.

spring 2018 (4-22)

every now and then
it is not now it is then
thenoh you appear

winter 2021 (2-16)

Paul Skuta

Philemon to Baucis

Let them gather
with leaves like hands,
hold in their hearts,
deeper, our days,
saving us for myth
which, anyway, stands
as long as love
and more than trees.

summer 1987

nights long
yet not long
cold mornings
doves' throats thicken with song
quickening
i swell like the tree
the breathing
of spring woman is on me

winter 2006

Spring woman,
you rose from me.
In the east you trailed your bright skirts
across the meadow.
I waited
while summer made the grasses high
and hid the way of your return.
To the west, another,
her skirt brown like the grasses,
her blanket red and yellow.
Spring woman,
my thoughts of you
are as the gathering birds.

summer 2009 (8-30)

Buffalo Hunt

Over now.
Better to have availed yourself
of more of the beast
as it staggered before you,
grunting and bellowing
after the chase,
taken from it more than
tongue and hair.
You fled though,
the red death smell of entrails,
the vulgarity of meat,
while accepting entirely
would have prevented degradation
and rendered both animals
deeply, eternally fertile.
Over now.
Done.

winter 2006 (2-19)

V
DEATH

O look so
me bod
(not m)y
d
(thank you
know god)
i.e.
d!

summer 1980 (8-22)

The season has descended
in an orange agony;
filament of worry
almost pulls the sky.
A panic of the grass
is summer's final industry.
Chill has stunned the tendril
and intensified the tree.

autumn 1982

J   (will)
h (u?)
        st
   old me
ev (wh)
        en (I) tu
all y (get)
CEE.

autumn 1980 (11-19)

The Dead

The Dead are not asleep;
The Dead are not in pain.
The Dead are not lost;
The Dead are not alone.
The Dead are not restless,
The Dead are not cold,
The Dead are not powerless,
The Dead are not afraid.
The Dead are not remorseful.
The Dead are not buried.
The Dead are not pitiful.
The Dead are not the dead.

winter 2009 (2-24)

we know that
night becomes day
and even (i know)
light becomes leaf
leaf light and
any can see
(but) love is all
(how) all is brief
yet (you see)
the great souls say
trustmeiknow
relinquish grief
(am i to kiss
whom or why now?
that you are
,you know). If

summer 2002 (7-21)

when meeting away from worry,
regarding with pity want,
not our names but we'll recall
our songs,
our purest smiles,
our youngest eyes,
our bravest hands remembered
of our remembered hearts
becoming our sweetest notes
as, at once and together,
we sing,
"hello hello, my soul."

summer 1988

Cloud Story

Once upon a time
a man saw a beautiful cloud
shaped like a fish
swimming in the sky.
He made a box
shaped like the fish
to keep the cloud in it.
The box was heavy.
When it fell out of the sky
and broke apart,
the cloud shaped like a fish
escaped
shaped like a bird.

spring 2019 (3-25)

Paul Skuta

You Are Here

Particle after particle,
body to body,
out of blackness, necessity
and boundless hope
we stream.
Photon after photon
we fade from one galaxy
to turn up twinkling
in another.

Back there
your curl the thickness
of a finger;
my finger
the thinness of a hair.
Here
it is my hair,
your finger.

Anyway, make a wish.
Blow them all out.
Happy Birthday,
Mother.

spring 1994 (3-27)

VI
THE INVISIBLE ROOM

The invisible one
in the invisible room
feels invisible walls
with invisible hands;
immersed in the ineffable answer,
silently it repeats the wordless question.

autumn 2009 (10-4)

disappearing exercise

I (breathe in) love You
(breathe out) love Me
We (breathe) love
i (breathe in) love you
(breathe out) love me
we (breathe) love
(i) breathe in love (you)
breathe out love (me)
(we) breathe love
(i) breathe in Love (you)
breathe out Love (me)
(we) breathe Love
breathe in Love
breathe out Love
breathe Love
breathe in
breathe out
Breathe

winter 2003 (2-26)

Three Airs

1

Man, the word.
Man, the body.
Note how each appears whole.
Upon close inspection, however,
both are seen to be dissolving:
one into paper,
one into space.

2

The core is dense
but not solid.
There are no solids,
only thought captured by gravity.

3

Birth is the contraction of heaven.
Life is the struggle with gravity.
Death is the little bang.

winter 2002 (1-5)

all the days hold hands
pulling uphill sliding down
but which day is first

autumn 2018 (11-17)

Geese

Many are gone
before you are counting;
the rest amaze you
with their wild calling.
Obscure and moon-pulled,
a final few.
Now where to go?
Now what to do?

autumn 1993 (10-31)

spider-mind spinning
memory with yet-to-be
catches just itself

autumn 2015 (9-7)

Paul Skuta

onetwothreebluejays
why must I count them threefour
threefourfivebluejays

winter 2019 (12-15)

the old man grew tired
he went into the forest
there he found a boy

winter 2019 (3-3)

yes, but dragonfly
battering against the glass,
the jar is open

summer 2018 (6-18)

Hexagram

each retreating wave
holds its souvenir of sand
each advancing wave

how the shore resists
which sand was which and which wave
how the shore accepts

winter 2003 (1-24)

Paul Skuta

as leaves down onto
down onto a lake as leaves
down onto as leaves

summer 1988

three leaves on the ground
the way perfectly revealed
five leaves on the ground

autumn 2005 (10-30)

wordless to see all
while in body—here and there
so not being gone

winter 2019 (2-22)

sublime to be gone
not in body—here or there
and so to be all

winter 2019 (2-23)

The Trees

cannot see me
but they sense me.
As I stand among them,
I need not see them.
Serenely we wait
to welcome the next one.

autumn 2017 (11-11)

Forever is it here
and never does it stay,
revealing itself
as it turns away.
Behold the chimera
of day and night,
sorrow and laughter,
wrong and right,
on whose wings
everything flies
as something is born
and something dies.

winter 2010 (12-5)

there it is balanced
a pinpoint on a pinpoint
everalwaysnow

spring 2018 (3-11)

In the song of birds
shall i stay in the world
and not be held;
in the wind
shall i again
find freedom.
My old age will be
the acorn falling;
in the snow dancing
will my rest be.
In love
shall i be born.

summer 2007 (8-4)

fly upon water
neither swimming nor walking
vanishes not wet

summer 2007 (7-7)